How Would Your Life Be if You Had Your Time and Money Issues Resolved and You Were Living Your Dream?

Dear Reader,

Does it ever seem like the more money you make, the less time you have to enjoy it? What would you do differently if you could change that situation? How do you suppose that might feel?

You undoubtedly work hard and enjoy a successful career or business. But like most people today, you're probably so busy that you can't seem to find enough time to spend with those you care most about, let alone enjoy your favorite activities.

Have you ever wanted things to ease up a bit so you could "stop and smell the roses"? After all, success isn't the end point; it's supposed to be a journey you enjoy along the way. Isn't that what you're working for?

The purpose of this book is to share with you what many dedicated people like you are doing to transition out of the craziness of the "rat race." Have you ever felt like saying, "I've had enough. Now it's my turn, and I'm going to do something about it"?

You're about to get a brief overview of an exciting, cutting edge business that you can manage from the comfort of your own home, without affecting your current occupational activities. It offers you the potential of generating a strong secondary income and beyond, while taking advantage of the latest economic trends and tax laws.

It combines the newest technology with a people-oriented, professional business development system that can help you accelerate your success. You can start associating with a community of experienced mentors and coaches, including those who have already resolved their time and money issues and are living their dreams, as well as those who are working toward those objectives. They can guide and help you to avoid making a lot of mistakes along the way, supporting you in reaching new levels of achievement.

So, take the next 60 minutes to read this enlightening book, and get rejuvenated. Welcome to a future that offers you the potential of gaining the additional time and money you may need to live your dream…and more.

All things start with a dream,

The Publisher

PS. This is one of the most important books we have ever published. Apply and share its stimulating ideas with others…and watch what happens!

Could *This* Be What You're Looking For?

Time and Money 2 Live Your Dream

Now You Can Create a Brighter Future by Profiting from the Expansive Growth of an Innovative Business

John Fuhrman

International Bestselling Author

A ***Possibility Press*** Book

Time and Money 2 Live Your Dream

Published by
Possibility Press
info@possibilitypress.com

Manufactured in the United States of America

— Contents —

"*Aspiring millionaires are best advised not to go to work for big corporations. In fact, 85% of America's million-aires own their own businesses...*"

—*US News and World Report*

— Introduction —

Could *This* Be What You're Looking For?

*"The successful person is
one who had the chance and took it"*
—Roger Babson—

Yes, it could well be! People throughout the world are taking advantage of the innovative business model briefly covered in this book. It's people teaming up with others who also want to resolve their time and money issues and live their dreams.

At one time, generating a substantial income from home had been something few people could do very successfully. But now you, too, can partake of the growing profits being generated by owning a home-managed business that's supported by a team of experienced business development mentors and coaches. They build "communities" of other home-managed business owners, as well as consumers, who purchase goods and services both online and via more traditional methods like catalogs and toll-free ordering.

Basically, you have three options regarding what you can do with this opportunity:

1) Ignore it and maintain the status-quo.
2) Be a consumer to save time and money.
3) Profit from its exciting growth, without affecting your current job or business.

Are you going to take advantage of this opportunity, or let it go by like you may have done with other opportunities in the past? You don't want to regret it later and say, "If only I had taken advantage of that opportunity when I first learned about it, I'd be so much further ahead today! Why didn't I do it?"

What if some people you know or hear about take advantage of it and run with it, and achieve more of their dreams and goals? Would you be sorry if you hadn't done so yourself?

Obviously, everyone, including those who are already making a great living, would like to have more time and money. But when an opportunity comes along to do just that, most people, unfortunately, aren't even made aware of it. It's not their fault. They just don't know about it, so they simply continue doing what they're doing, even though they might want things to change. Anticipating things will soon get better, they keep busy following the same routine, not realizing they could also be following their dream.

As you might expect, the results are predictable. If they don't do something about it, things usually stay the same or even go downhill. For example, they could find themselves involved in a layoff or rightsizing. But now, here's a chance to guard against events like that from negatively affecting your lifestyle.

So, what four things do most people with their time and money issues resolved have in common?

1) They come from all walks of life.
2) They seized opportunity when it knocked.
3) They're no more intelligent or better qualified than you or me.
4) They made a decision and took appropriate action.

So, how can you become one of them? Read this book. Learn about a vehicle you can use to help you resolve your time and money issues, get out of debt, build more financial security, and live the life you desire.

Do you know how to generate a strong secondary income from home without being a techno-wizard or business genius? You're about to get a brief overview of an exciting business model that can help you do so. You'll learn how you can possibly become a part of it and diversify your income with it.

By following a proven business development system, guided by a dedicated support team of mentors and coaches, coupled with the speed and power of online and offline business capabilities—you, too, have a new opportunity to increase your prosperity.

Obviously, only you have the final say in how you choose to live the rest of your life. Would you like to make an even more informed decision about your future? This book can help you do that.

Can you recall your childhood dreams where you could be, do, and have anything you wanted? How did you imagine your life would be as an adult? If you're not quite where you'd like to be in life, here's an opportunity for you to do something about it.

Have you noticed a decline in shoppers at the local malls, and even store closings, because of more people doing business and shopping from home?

Do you realize that the Post Office, UPS, FedEx, and other package delivery services are enjoying significant increases in business, because of more people doing business and shopping from home?

Are you aware that there's a continuing decrease in the time people spend watching primetime television, as millions choose to spend increasing amounts of time online?

Fortunately, you don't have to be a computer wizard or business genius to take advantage of this opportunity. It's a high-tech/high-touch business, where people are the most important part. It's people using technology, both low-tech toll-free catalog ordering and high-tech online components, helping others leverage their way to greater success. They build relationships—the most valuable asset of any business—offline, while using the latest technology online.

You don't need to create a website; it's already been done! This and other technical aspects have been taken care of. You simply use the site already developed and maintained by your business development support team.

You may also find your children eager to help you with your business. It would be a fun, educational experience for them, and draw you all closer together!

Yes, a golden opportunity is knocking on your door; loud and clear. Go ahead and seize it! Open your mind and unlock your vision for a brighter future. Once and for all, accelerate your progress toward resolving your time and money issues and living your dream.

Read *Time and Money 2 Live Your Dream* and discover the possibilities—for you!

— 1 —
So, How Can You Benefit from the Expansive Growth of This Innovative Business?

"Some great people are leaders and others
are more lucky, in the right place at the right time.
I'd put myself in the latter category."
— Steve Wozniak —

Bill Gates, founder of Microsoft, richest man in the world and well-known philanthropist, along with his wife, Melinda, wouldn't be where they are today if it weren't for his innovative technology.

Michael Dell, business innovator and founder of Dell Computers, said that, "It's through curiosity and looking at opportunities in new ways that we've always mapped out our path at Dell. There's always an opportunity to make a difference."

Jeff Bezos, founder of Amazon.com, said that, "If you do build a great experience, customers tell each other about that. Word of mouth is very powerful."

Steven Jobs and Steve Wozniak, founders of Apple Computers, started the personal computer revolution and became "zillionaires." Jobs, who also co-founded Pixar Animation, said that "Our belief was that if we kept putting great products in front of customers, they would continue to open their wallets."

"Sure, those people are on top of their game, but how can that help me increase my prosperity?" you ask. Well, you're about to learn about an exciting business opportunity that can help you do that. It uses the technology and ideas they and others have developed. And it could help take you where you want to go, whether it's to realize your wildest dreams, or earn just a couple hundred extra dollars a month. It's up to you.

Fortunately, someone thought highly enough of you and your abilities to lend you this book. Perhaps they noticed something about you that you may not have seen in yourself.

It could have been something you said. Maybe it was your enthusiasm that caught their attention.

Or, perhaps, they consider you a friend worthy of sharing good news with.

But regardless of the reason they shared this book with you, you can feel complimented they did. After you've finished reading it, you might notice, more than ever, the news stories about the phenomenal growth of online business-to-consumer spending. You may also start becoming more aware of the trend toward home-managed business ownership.

According to Paul Zane Pilzer, world-renowned economist and former economic advisor in two US Presidential administrations, ten million people, in the US alone, will become millionaires over the next ten years. He believes many of them will be home-managed business owners who share, or teach, others about what they have to offer, while also utilizing the web.

As you know, the web is certainly a convenient tool for making personal purchases, but it's also a wonderful tool for business. As Pilzer suggests, it's a part of the business model discussed in this book. Not only can people save time and money from the comfort of their own homes when they shop, but now they can also earn money while more efficiently operating a home-managed business.

What a great scenario!

More importantly, you'll begin to see how you could possibly take advantage of a dynamic business opportunity, that's on the cutting edge of what's happening in the marketplace. What you won't get, though, is something for nothing. This is not a get-rich-quick scheme. There are no guarantees that this is even what you're looking for.

But, *what if it is?*

Pilzer goes on to emphasize that, "As powerful as the Internet is, it hasn't replaced the one-on-one, personal function..., and it never will. Business is about serving other people. The better you are at giving people something that improves their lives, the more successful you are and the more money you make."

The main component of this innovative business model reflects Pilzer's thinking. It has been developed to give people, from all walks of life, a chance to get in on the action. But just like any worthwhile endeavor, the rewards go to those who earn them based on the effectiveness of the time and effort expended.

Unfortunately, some people you may know are under the illusion that they can keep doing the same things, and somehow their time and money issues will magically resolve themselves. But this is a dangerous belief that can lead to a lifetime of disappointment and regret.

The key factor here is that we all get what we focus on. Whether we realize it or not, we are where we are in life because that's what we've focused on.

Isn't that the truth?

Yes, everyone focuses on something, and that's what they get, provided they persist long enough. So, to resolve any time and money issues you may have and build more financial security, you might want to consider focusing more on doing that!

For example, whoever focuses on watching TV sitcoms will know all about the characters and stories. But that's not going to make them more financially secure. Whereas, if they would invest that same time in this opportunity, they would have the potential to resolve their time and money issues.

Dreams and goals form our vision of the future, which is what the most successful people focus on. Pursuing them more wholeheartedly will give you a sense of satisfaction and vitality, like nothing else in life can. You will be more pleased than ever, and have a greater feeling of accomplishment in the process of achieving them. You'll also have a happier, more rewarding life.

Yes, this home-managed business is expanding! Don't let its growth pass you by. Fortunately, the steps you can take in order to profit from its growth have all been carefully laid out, paving the way for your increased success.

Your next step is simply to finish reading this book.

— 2 —

Why You Might Want to Learn More About This Opportunity

"It is insane to depend on your employer for security."
—*Worth* Magazine—

So, what's the first thing you need to have in order to get different results in your life? As you've undoubtedly experienced, it's a strong enough desire for something you don't already have—a goal, dream, or objective that you have yet to accomplish.

If you're satisfied with your life the way it is, that's great! Why do anything other than what you're already doing? Why bother, if your life is already exactly the way you dreamed it would be?

Now, some may say, "Don't talk to me about dreams." That's okay. But if they honestly think for a moment about why they do things, they'll realize it's because they have a desire, or dream, to get a certain result. That's all we're saying here. A dream or a goal, as you undoubtedly know, is truly the driving force behind anyone making a positive change, even if it's simply the hope that next year will be better!

For example, you probably have a job or business to pay your bills, maintain your current lifestyle, and afford some of life's pleasures, right?

The sad reality is, though, that at least 70% of the population dislikes going to work! How about you?

Do you go to your job or business only because you believe you have to? Or is it simply because, until now, you haven't been made aware of any other viable options?

Maybe you have never even considered the possibility of doing something outside your current occupation to give yourself a better lifestyle. Perhaps you haven't considered the idea that you could personally generate income from home.

What does your financial picture look like? Are you out of debt yet? Are you concerned that you may not have enough money for a carefree retirement, after you've put your children through college? Forty-four million people, in the US alone, are facing under-funded retirements. Don't depend on your employer for a secure one.

Are you all stressed out and, yet, still not getting ahead financially as well as you'd like, even though you're working overtime, have a second job, or just got promoted?

Are you fed up with your boss, co-workers, associates, or employees, and how they treat you, each other, and the people you all serve? Does it ever seem like your job or business owns you rather than you owning it?

Do you realize that hundreds of thousands of people lose their jobs every year because of new technology and manufacturing jobs being relocated out of the country? And you've, no doubt, observed that entire industries are disappearing as new technology replaces the old.

For example, the audiotape industry is rapidly disappearing. CDs, PCs, MP3 players, and iPods have pretty much taken over. DVDs are replacing videotapes. Computers have replaced typewriters, and digital HDTV is replacing dot matrix TV. Cell phones and wireless e-mail devices have revolutionized the convenience of personal communications and virtually eliminated payphones. Digital cameras, in conjunction with computers and printers, are replacing traditional film cameras and photo processing. PDAs are replacing traditional handwritten date books and planners. Satellite radio and TV are growing in popularity. The world is going increasingly high-tech.

While the economy looks strong, it's primarily so because of rapidly increasing consumer debt, which has exceeded an astonishing $10 trillion in the US alone, with only 1% of the average family's income going to savings. People, more than ever, are buying with borrowed money, living on borrowed time. In fact, over one-and-a-half million people filed for bankruptcy last year and there has been a 2.3% drop in family income since 2001.

Does it seem like your life is being consumed by paying bills? Have you ever felt overwhelmed by the time and money it takes servicing your debt load, while feeling a growing sense of financial insecurity?

Have you, or has anyone you know of, ever been downsized? Has your company, or others you may have heard of, ever merged or been acquired in a hostile takeover? Has your company, or any you know of, ever relocated or closed facilities, because of cheaper labor abroad? Have you, or has anyone you know of, ever been demoted?

Well, the great news is, you can rise above all of these challenges by profiting from the expansive growth of this home-managed business. Instead of worrying about what might happen, you can work on being happier and growing toward becoming more financially secure. They're profiting from home by building this innovative business.

Would you like to go fishing, boating, or golfing, or participate in some other sport or hobby you enjoy, whenever you feel like it?

Would you like to spend more time with your family and, perhaps, travel more, have more money to spend, and stay as long as you wish?

Would you find it gratifying to give more generously to your place of worship, and to charities and causes you believe in?

How about retiring early from your job or business?

But, no matter what your desires may be, the key question is simply this...

> "How would you like to have all the time and money you need to do whatever you want to do whenever you want to do it?"

Now, all of this may seem like hype or just plain wishful thinking. That's certainly understandable. Perhaps you feel this way because you may not personally know anyone who has both their time and money issues totally resolved.

If you're like most people, you associate primarily with others who are at your own socio-economic level, as high as that may be. Therefore, you may not have any collegues who could introduce you to a role model of greater success who would *also* help you move on, except perhaps the person who lent you this book!

When you stop and think about it, most people who have the time to do what they want to do probably don't have the money. Conversely, most people who have the money probably don't have the time to enjoy it!

But—*for you*—it doesn't have to be that way!

There are those who have "set themselves up." They took advantage of this opportunity when it was presented to them, and developed it to the point where they have resolved their time and money issues. Many of them started when they were better off than most people, while some were financially strapped.

Today, there are people everywhere who are making their dreams come true by conveniently managing their own business from home, often with their family participating.

When would you like to join them?

What's your biggest dream or goal? Are you now working toward it? Do you want it seriously enough to put forth the extra time and effort needed to accomplish it?

"Don't put all your eggs in one basket," is a sage piece of advice we've all heard. That's how the wealthy operate. They don't rely on just one source of income.

This opportunity gives you the chance to diversify, by developing a strong secondary income. At a minimum, this business model can help you save some time and money.

Wouldn't it be great to have another source of income, equal to or greater than what your current occupation provides? Wouldn't that enable you to considerably accelerate your success? Then it wouldn't matter if you lost or left your job, or had to sell or close your current business, now would it?

Wouldn't that give you greater peace of mind?

Would you like to open the door to an even better life for you and your family? If so, keep in mind what some wealthy people say...

"Remember, if your outgo exceeds your income, your upkeep becomes your downfall. Don't live on borrowed money. Get out of debt so you can be in the position to pay cash for whatever it is you need or want. Finance and interest charges not only eat away at your potential for a secure future but they also add stress that you can negatively affect your health, well-being, and relationships.

"Don't just work hard for a living; also work smart for a lifestyle. Team up with like-minded, positive-thinking, proactive people who can help you do that."

— 3 —

Shoulda, Coulda, Woulda, and "If Only I Had Done So…"

"The follies which a person regrets most in their life are those which they didn't commit to when they had the opportunity."
—Helen Rowland—

I once read an interesting story about a man who went to work for Microsoft in its early days. His pay was very low. Even so, he had saved up and bought $2,100 worth of stock because he believed in the company's future. Without buying any additional stock, he became a multi-millionaire in less than ten years! Would you have done what he did if you had been given the same opportunity? Or would you have passed on it, only to regret it later?

No one but you can decide what you're going to do with this opportunity. Like the man who bought the Microsoft stock, when you have a dream, believe enough in this business model and what it has to offer you, and take appropriate action, you could profit handsomely in the coming years.

Review the rest of this book with an open, inquisitive mind. Then ask the person who shared it with you for more information.

Also have him or her introduce you to some of the successful people on the mentoring and coaching team who may live in your area. Meeting them can help you determine the right thing for you to do.

As you know, to achieve different results in your life, you need to do something else that can give you those results. In fact, people in the personal and professional development arena often define insanity as "continuing to do the same things while expecting different results"!

Do you know anyone who does that?

What will your life be like in the next two to five years if you keep doing what you're doing?

How can you tell?

Just look at somebody who's been doing what you do two to five years longer than you have. That'll probably give you a pretty good idea of where you'll be in life if you don't do something that can give you what you really want.

Remember this...

If you continue doing what you've always done, you'll just continue to have what you've always had, or maybe even less! Nothing is likely to improve by itself, and you may not get what you want out of life. And even though your occupational income may increase, will you have the time you would really like to have to enjoy your life and your family?

Are you pleased with what you see down the road? If not, ask yourself these two simple questions...

1) If you're not going to take advantage of this opportunity to work toward resolving your time and money issues, then what will you do to live your dream?

2) If you don't do something now, will you be sorry later?

"**L**ife moves on, whether we act as cowards or heroes. Life has no other discipline to impose if we would but realize it, than to accept life unquestioningly. Everything we shut our eyes to, everything we run away from, everything we deny, denigrate or despise, serves to defeat us in the end. What seems different, scary, or challenging, can be a source of beauty, joy, and strength, when faced with an open mind. Every moment is a golden one for those who have the vision to recognize it as such."

—Henry Miller

— 4 —

Ch-Ch-Ch-Changes — The Only Thing Constant in Life Is Change

"Since changes are going on anyway, the great thing is to learn enough about them so that we will be able to lay hold of them and turn them in the direction of our desires. Conditions and events are neither to be fled from nor passively acquiesced in; they are to be utilized and directed."
—John Dewey—

When I was a young boy, we would visit my grandparents. One of the things I remember most was mowing the lawn. And since they had a postage stamp-sized yard, they didn't need a power mower.

I'd cut the grass with an old-time push mower, the kind with the long spiral blades that turned with the wheels as you pushed. And even though there was no grass to pick up and bag, my grandmother would give me a dollar when I was done.

Today, things are different. There are more options: self-propelled, push power, riding, mulching, and rear-bagging mowers, plus weed wackers, leaf blowers, and more.

Yet, as you know, even with all the improvements in lawn care technology, one essential ingredient still remains; someone has to operate the equipment. These machines and tools simply cannot do the work by themselves. They need the human element, the high-touch of people.

People always need to actively participate in the process, or the job never gets done.

The evolution of the computer and communications devices has followed much the same trail. From a massive multi-room piece of complicated electronics and machinery, to simple units that can now be held in the palm of your hand. And who knows what's next?

Computers are getting faster and "smarter" with each generation, and can do virtually anything the user might imagine. For example, a computer typed the original manuscript for this book, while I spoke the words. Once again, a person has to add his or her high-touch to the technology, or nothing happens.

All of these innovations sound like science fiction, don't they? And, of course, they were at one time. As you are well aware, new electronic devices, or tools, are being created every day, and they are becoming more available and affordable than ever. These technological marvels are also getting more user-friendly with each new model or program. They are designed to make our lives easier by helping us get more done in less time.

But just as with lawn care equipment, a person is needed to control all the technological power. Someone needs to first turn the tools on, before they can even be used, let alone assist us in reaching our full potential.

That's how it is with this business model; people are definitely the mainstay. They need to use the tools and other resources available in order to benefit from what they can do.

Would you like that someone to be you?

Is there potential for you to resolve your time and money issues and live your dream with this opportunity?

Absolutely!

The knowledge to help you succeed is readily available through a committed team of mentors and coaches. Just ask them to show you the way.

But, as you'll undoubtedly agree, the only way you can build a successful business, of any kind, is to first have a strong enough desire to make some changes in your life, and then take appropriate action.

As the saying goes...

"If you want some things to change in your life, you need to change some things in your life!"

— 5 —

Why Would You Want to Embrace the Tremendous Power of This Opportunity?

"The secret to success in life is for a person to be ready for their opportunity when it comes."
—Benjamin Disraeli—

If you're not serious about taking full advantage of this opportunity, you might be making a big mistake. However, by doing so, you could gain the competitive edge you need to reach your next level of success.

Businesses that don't embrace new technologies may well go out of business. For example, according to various sources, online sales are growing 14-20% a year. By 2010, this sector of the economy could account for 10% of all retail sales, reach $329 billion in the US, alone, and top $1 trillion globally.

Yes, your own business, managed from home, enabled by both an online infrastructure and the offline support of a dedicated team of mentors and coaches, could be the ideal way for you to accelerate your success. The question is, "When are you going to start taking advantage of the tremendous potential that's waiting for you?"

The predictions you've just read are based on current economic trends and the latest technological developments. But as great as they are, none of them can possibly be of any benefit to you without one very important ingredient—you!

New technology, especially to the non-technical person, may seem like a miracle. But, coupled with appropriate support, it can offer you a more promising future only when you seize the opportunity and run with it. Otherwise, it won't do you any good.

No doubt about it, today's technology, coupled with this innovative business model, is making it easier for more people to prosper. But, if you don't let anyone know you're a part of it, all the technology in the world can't help you resolve your time and money issues, or build a more secure financial future.

To maximize the possibilities you could realize to make your life more like you want it to be, you need to have easy access to a team of mentors and coaches who can assist you.

To benefit, you need to take action and share this powerful opportunity with others.

For example, if Edison hadn't told anyone about the light bulb he had just invented and, instead, had kept it to himself, what do you suppose would have become of it?

Nothing!

All high-tech developments and opportunities are worthless without the high-touch of people.

In fact, the best way you or anyone else can succeed at anything new is to get help from an experienced mentor or coach. Then take action and share whatever it is you are doing with others.

If you don't do something to enhance your potential, you'll be standing by the roadside watching others pass you by. Then, two to five years from now, you might say, "If only I had invested some of my time in that business when I was first made aware of it, I'd be so much further ahead! Why didn't I do it?"

Using the appropriate tools is certainly a step in the right direction. And through the process of trial and error, you might eventually be able to use them to their fullest potential.

But what if you could quickly learn what you need to know to get started? Why search for years to discover the real capabilities of this exciting business model? Well, you can speed up the process...

After you read this book, ask the person who lent it to you what you could do next. If they're also new at it, don't worry. They're connected with the right people, and can refer you to business leaders with the experience and knowledge to help you succeed. But it's up to you to ask for assistance.

So, why would you want to embrace the tremendous power of this opportunity, and share it with others? Because it can help you to develop a more substantial financial foundation and live more of the life you truly desire.

If you keep it to yourself, it's not going to do you or anyone else any good. As Bill Gates of Microsoft says, "What I do best is share my enthusiasm!"

So start sharing your enthusiasm by spreading the word...

— 6 —
Now, Let's Review the Basic Keys to Maximizing Your Success

"Teamwork is the ability to work
together toward a common vision. The ability to
direct individual accomplishments toward organizational
objectives. It is the fuel that allows common people
to attain uncommon results."
—Andrew Carnegie—

Everyone who becomes a part of the team has the chance to work with people who have become more successful. And, while everyone has their own business, no one needs to figure everything out for themselves.

So how can you most effectively start accelerating the resolution of your time and money issues and live more of your dreams? Follow a proven business development system; one that has already been meticulously thought out, and is helping countless others reach a new level of living. This would include creating more positive relationships, having a better outlook on life, and a greater sense of accomplishment.

So, what are the basic keys to maximizing your success? Simply this: Focus more intensely on your dreams and goals, continue growing personally and professionally, build more mutually beneficial relationships, use the latest high-tech tools to greater advantage, and share this book with others who want to do the same.

By using this superb business model you can create a strong secondary income, and become more successful than you otherwise might have been. Thankfully, there's a willing team of capable people who can help you do that.

After all, *no one can succeed alone!*

Invest time in the people around you, including those you know and the new people you meet, taking a genuine interest in their dreams and goals, and you can gain tremendous rewards.

As the old Chinese proverb says, "If you want prosperity in a year, grow a crop. If you want prosperity in ten years, grow trees. But, if you want prosperity for a lifetime, grow people."

It's only when working in concert with others, who are going in the same direction, that truly great success can occur.

Just think about all the famous successful people you have ever heard of, for example, owners of athletic teams, corporate CEOs, or other well-known wealthy individuals.

What do all these people have in common?

In every single case, you'll find that they have surrounded themselves with other forward-thinking, like-minded people—employees, teammates, group members, associates, or others—who are also serious about achieving more success in that arena.

The opportunity you are now considering gives you the chance to work with others to accomplish more of your dreams and goals, without a big investment or any particular talents or gifts. The main thing you need is desire.

You can receive all the support you want and need. There are dedicated people, informational materials, books, CDs, DVDs, seminars, and the like, to help you grow to any level of success you may wish to achieve.

Now, while you would be in business for yourself, you wouldn't be in business by yourself. There's a team of professional people available to guide and help you, as long as you're willing to do your part in making it happen.

Remember, all true success is the result of people working together. That's the cornerstone of what makes this such a solid opportunity.

Generally speaking, most successful people will not take the time to tell you or show you what they did to become successful, let alone help you succeed like they did. Most wealthy people just won't share the secrets of their success. That's unfortunate.

However, the successful people you could be teaming up with here have come from virtually every job or career imaginable, and they can help you accelerate your success. They've been where you are and they have empathy for and understand what you may be experiencing. Even though you may already be making $100,000 a year, or more, they realize that the higher your compensation package is, the more your company "owns" you! Your personal time has, most likely, been compromised to the point where you may not be seeing much of your spouse or family.

Unlike many other opportunities, what you have here is a proven business development system, designed to help those who ask for it. It's people helping people, while using technology to leverage their success.

As the saying goes, *"Ask and you shall receive."*

"So, why in the world would someone who's already wealthy and successful in a different arena want to help *me*?" you may ask. Now let's just think about that for a minute. For example, why would a star athlete keep on playing the game? Why would someone who's made millions keep on going?

Why do they keep going, even though they have their time and money problems solved?

It could be for any number of reasons: They love what they do; they enjoy associating with and helping others in their field; they give back to their communities; they go on to support charities and establish foundations; they use their excess wealth to make investments and set up or purchase other businesses; or they do whatever else they choose, because they have the time and money to do so.

It'll be heartwarming when you discover that the leaders on the success team you're considering being a part of enjoy helping others, no matter how successful they may already be. If you doubt it, ask the person who lent you this book to introduce you to some of them, or to put you in touch with someone who can...

Then decide for yourself!

—7—

Time and Money and the Real "Secret" of the Wealthy

*"The plain truth is this: You cannot
count on your employer, the state, or the economy to
provide for your future security. It is
entirely in your hands."*
—*Fortune* Magazine—

W hen asked what their main concerns in life are, most people include, "Time and money"—the *lack* of time and money! There always seems to be too much month left at the end of the money. As a result, people often work long hours or take a second job in an attempt to make up for it.

If that doesn't work, they may go into or get deeper in debt, making their financial situation even worse. But as soon as they begin catching up on their bills, they may realize they've created yet another undesirable situation: There's little or no time left to spend with the most important people in their lives or to do the things they'd really love to do.

It can be a vicious cycle, *with no end in sight.*

While the bills get paid, their quality of life suffers, as does that of their families, who rarely see them. Everybody seems all stressed out and generally not very happy. They feel like they're on a treadmill, running "a million miles an hour," getting nowhere fast. Have you ever had that experience or know of anyone who has? Is that any kind of way to live?

Having a business that's managed from home enables people to get on the track to change all of that. When they purchase various consumer products and other goods and services online, or via catalogs that are available through their business, the very first thing they'll save is time. The time spent going to various stores, to get many of those same items, is now theirs to do something else with!

As Ben Franklin said, "Time is money." But as you share this business with others who team up with you, that adage can, in time, begin changing to "Time *earns* money."

Those who understand the true potential here may join you. As you'll learn, you can also generate income based on what they purchase and the businesses they develop.

Continue repeating that process, and you have the potential for earning the best form of income there is, ongoing, the kind you receive for work you've already done. This is the real "secret" of the wealthy. Instead of trading time for money, like most people do when they work a job, they have money coming in even when they're not working. They've typically created a scenario that uses an appropriate vehicle which allows this to occur.

Share this business with enough people who also take advantage of it, and your income from it can continue to grow. Unlike it is with a job, though, you wouldn't be subjected to demotions, layoffs, downsizings, plant shutdowns, or a forced retirement. It's a wonderful example of what time and effort invested now can potentially do for your future.

When your income gets big enough, you could move on from being concerned about the pitfalls of working at a job or another business. You can be compensated for your past efforts as long as your business has a strong growing foundation.

Wouldn't that be great?

More importantly, though, you owe it to yourself and your family to at least explore this viable option, and discover what it can potentially do for you and your lifestyle. You'll probably be pleasantly surprised and pleased by what you find.

As others see you becoming even happier and more successful, they may approach you to find out why that is so. When they do, simply lend them this book and let it do its job—for you! If they're still not sure, you might suggest they just try the business before making any decisions. Lend them some of these books and suggest that they simply share them with a few friends and acquaintances…and watch what happens.

What could result is a chance for you, and those assisting you, to meet with those people. They, as a group, can then learn more about this business model and its potential—all at the same time.

If, after that, some say they have no further interest, that's fine. You haven't lost a thing. But, unfortunately, they have! Just keep going. Who knows? They may team up with you later.

There are certainly those who don't want to miss out on an opportunity that they can use to improve their lifestyle. There are people everywhere who would like to address their time and money challenges and live their dream.

You can count on it….

There are people everywhere, at all levels of accomplishment, who would just love to have more time and money to live their dream. They'd love to have the potential of an ongoing income that comes in whether they're working or not—the real "secret" of the wealthy!

You can be sure of that!

"When building a team, I always search for people who love to win. If I can't find any of those, I look for people who hate to lose."

—H. Ross Perot

— 8 —

Share This Opportunity and Leverage Your Way to Greater Financial Security

"...word-of-mouth [sharing] accelerates online to an almost unfathomable degree...with the click of a mouse, now people can tell thousands...our business recognizes the shift of power toward the [people]."
— Jeff Bezos, Founder and CEO, Amazon.com —

Have you ever seen a really good movie and liked it so much that you recommended it to others? Of course you have. But you didn't get paid for doing that, did you? You helped the movie producers, actors, and theater owners get rich. But you didn't even make a cent!

Now, how would you like to have the potential of generating income from your recommendations? Simply start sharing this book with others, and you can accomplish two things...

First, you'll find the people who would like to have the time and money to live their dreams. Second, you'll also be showing them the rudiments of what they need to start doing to begin building their own business.

When that happens, you can begin getting paid, as long as you are part of the team, because you were the one who recommended the opportunity to people who took advantage of it!

Just start sharing this book with others. They can then follow your example with the people they know and with whom they come in contact.

The big benefit is that you, and those who team up with you, can use the power of this book and this business model to work for both you and them. It's a real win-win situation, and an efficient use of the tools and support available to help you.

You'll also save time, which is probably the first thing you may want more of in your busy life. Increasing your income is certainly a wonderful, marvelous thing. But what good does it do you unless you have the time to enjoy it?

This book simply introduces people to the opportunity, covers some of the basics, and answers a few common questions. If they want more information, it's available. Those who understand the potential and want to team up with others who can help them become more successful, may want to take advantage of the opportunity—and call you!

You come back into the picture only after they express interest or want to learn more. If they don't, you just move on!

You're looking for people who really want to make their dreams come true or, perhaps, just want to save some time and money, and everybody in between. This book is simply a tool that can help you spread the word about the opportunity it briefly describes.

For those who want to maintain the status quo, that's fine. It's certainly their choice. As the saying goes, "You can lead a horse to water, but you can't make him drink." He's got to be thirsty! You're simply looking for some "thirsty" people.

Sharing this book with others will save you time and money. It eliminates the extra work you would otherwise have to do with people who may not be interested anyway.

Not spending any time on someone who would say "no" is a great advantage. It's one of the most positive things that can happen when building any business—you're not wasting your precious time.

Now understand, there are three possible outcomes from sharing this book and the opportunity it describes:

1) They won't be interested in anything presented.
2) They would like to save time and money.
3) They are also interested in creating a strong secondary income, or beyond, or perhaps earning just enough extra money to pay off some bills.

Remember, just because someone doesn't want to save time and money or move on when you do, doesn't mean they won't want to later on. Then, too, some people may criticize you and even try to hold you back! But don't let that bother you. It can happen.

Deep down inside, though, they'll probably respect you. Furthermore, their attitude or circumstances could change at any time, and they just might give you a call! No matter what, though, the more people you share this opportunity with, without getting hung up on any individual response, the faster your business can grow, and the more success you can achieve.

Now, ask yourself, "How many really happy people do I know?" If you're like most, you'll probably say, "Very few!"

There are people everywhere, no matter what their income level may be or how prosperous they may appear, who are going to bed every night, hoping and praying for an opportunity like this to come along. They could be in debt, sick and tired of the grind of their job or business, or just looking for something new to do—and you could help them!

Sharing this business opportunity could be one of the nicest things you do for someone. And, as in sharing or giving anything to anybody, or in doing a good deed, that's something you can feel good about. You've extended the hand of friendship.

How anybody responds to your good gesture is no reflection on you. It just depends on them, their situation, and their attitude. It depends on how they feel about themselves, on where they are in life, what they're doing now, and where they want to go.

Share this business opportunity because you believe it can help others, regardless of what you think they might think, say, or do about it. It simply doesn't matter. Some people will be grateful, while others may simply be afraid to admit they could use some help. That's just human nature.

The point is, don't be concerned about how any particular person responds. All that matters is what you say and do. It's what you believe taking advantage of this opportunity could do for you and your family that counts the most.

There are millions of people who are interested in saving more time and money and many who are also ready to move on. There are people everywhere who would welcome the right opportunity, and you could be the one to share it with them! Isn't it wonderful knowing you could make a positive difference in other people's lives?

Since time is money and time can earn money, as described earlier, it's essential to invest some time now if you want the potential of getting more back later, with "interest." It's a basic law of success. While we all have only 24 hours a day, when you share this opportunity with enough people, who in turn do the same thing, you can begin multiplying what you accomplish. That's leverage.

This business can work for you, somewhat like a corporation that becomes more profitable as it grows. Economies of scale and increasing productivity benefit the corporation, leading to higher profits.

But, unlike a corporation, you don't have any employees or their associated problems, because everyone is in their own business!

As shipping magnate J. Paul Getty, the world's richest man when he was alive, said, "I'd rather have 1% of the results of 100 men's [and women's] efforts than 100% of the results of just my own efforts."

You'll be enabled to leverage your time and multiply your results, by sharing and teaming up with other people, without having to hire them!

Share this opportunity with others, and you have the potential of leveraging your way to greater financial security and more free time. It's only when you work as a team with other people that you can become more successful than you already are. Working in concert with others forms the basis for creating a solid business capable of generating increasing income for you and your family.

This could be the key to getting on the road to resolving your time and money issues—*and living your dream*

— 9 —

So, Why Is Movement More Important than Motivation?

"The heights by great men [and women]
reached and kept were not attained by sudden flight.
But they, while their companions slept, were
toiling upward in the night."
— Henry Wadsworth Longfellow —

Now that you've read this far, you probably have a new and exciting sense of what's possible for you with this opportunity. Apparently, the person you received this book from saw something in you that told them you could benefit from this—*if you choose to.*

Have you begun dreaming about how much better your future could be? This is certainly an important first step. Are you motivated by what you have learned so far, and believe that what you envision is achievable?

> That's great if that's how you feel. But you need to be honest with yourself. That's not enough! You can feel motivated all you want and accomplish nothing more than having grand wishes. Or you can see this as your best chance to create an even better life, and start making some things happen.

Whether you totally understand this opportunity, or not, is less important than going forward with what you do understand. You can learn more about it as you go along.

For example, like starting a new job, getting married, or becoming a new parent, you begin these activities without knowing much about them. You just learn as you go. If everyone would wait until they knew everything about something new before they began doing it, no one would accomplish anything in life.

Your enthusiasm and actually sharing this opportunity with others is much more important than knowing all the details. You're excitedly going somewhere new and that's what can attract others to team up with you.

When the people you're sharing this opportunity with see that it can help them, they'll be more inclined to be interested. After all, nobody wants to miss out on a good thing.

Perhaps that's why you may want to get back to the person you received this book from.

The advanced technology and online infrastructure you would have access to is the latest available. And the business development system and team of qualified mentors and coaches that can help you achieve what you desire would be your foundation for greater success in life. It's people helping people work toward achieving their objectives so they can make their dreams come true.

The support team, along with the power of this business model, gives you tremendous potential. And since people and relationships are paramount, you never have to let the technology concern you. It's simply a tool to help you succeed—faster!

However, sharing the opportunity with others who team up with you is the main key to your success!

This book enables you to easily get started. All you need to do is finish reading it, and contact the person who shared it with you.

If you have no interest, simply give this book back to that person. Or, if you wish, pass it on to someone else you may know or meet who may welcome an opportunity to make his or her life better. He or she may call you or the person who lent you this book, as you may prefer. Who knows? They may want to get started right away!

However, if you think there might be something in this for you, ask for more information. And be sure to find out what to do next.

Regardless of where you are now in life, if you're not quite where you'd like to be, there is only one solution—you need to do something different!

If you want to be successful with this opportunity, just begin sharing it with other people. After all, surveys show that 95% of all people would like to have a business of their own. They may just need someone to show them the way.

And that someone could be—*you!*

So, why is movement more important than motivation?

It's simply what people *do* that counts!

— 10 —

Get the Best Advice You Can and Be Sure to Watch Out for Excuses!

"Keep away from people who try to belittle your ambitions. Small people always do that, but the really great make you feel that you, too, can become great."
— Mark Twain —

We benefit most by observing and learning from those who are more successful than we are. If you can meet someone who is successful in this endeavor, wouldn't it make sense to ask them how they did it and learn how you can too?

Remember the expression, "Give a man a fish, and he'll eat for a day. But, show him *how* to fish, and he'll eat for a lifetime"? Wouldn't it be great to be able to "fish" better than you already do, by learning from somebody who knows how?

Now, who's likely to give the best advice to someone who's seriously considering a business opportunity? Wouldn't you suggest that they consult with someone who's actually successful in that field, rather than someone who just has an opinion about it?

Yes, most people prefer learning from an experienced person. But, amazingly, some people sabotage their success by doing the opposite!

> What is baffling, is that there are some people who will look at an opportunity and then "consult" with a friend. Now mind you, that while their friend may be well-intended and have considerable expertise in their own field of endeavor, they may have no experience in any kind of business, let alone something as cutting edge as this. Incredibly, some people will still follow their so-called advice! The problem, of course, is that this will cause them to lose out on a potentially tremendous future. How sad...

If you want good financial advice, wouldn't it make the most sense to go to someone who is more financially successful than you are? You wouldn't even think of going to someone who is heavily in debt, broke, or just filed for bankruptcy, now, would you? Of course not!

Do yourself a favor; examine and evaluate this opportunity closely. Be sure to get all the facts, the real facts, from those who are successful in this arena.

Ask the person who lent you this book when and where you could attend a briefing or seminar.

Ask to be introduced to a variety of people from all walks of life. While many are probably just starting out, some will have already achieved great levels of success and affluence. Ask them why they took advantage of this opportunity, what they think about its potential for you, and how you could become successful at it too.

Never rely on opinions, hearsay, innuendoes, or excuses. And don't let anyone hold you back from doing what you need to do. After all, no one else is going to pay your bills or advance your lifestyle, except you!

There are people who, deep down inside, would honestly like more success. But, unfortunately, they sabotage it by making excuses, usually without even realizing it. It's just become a habit.

They tell themselves they don't want to learn how to "fish" any better then they already do, simply because they may fear change. That's too bad. This attitude is what keeps them from ever getting what they really want out of life.

Such people often complain but never do anything about it. They may say, "We're doing okay," or even "We're doing great." But what does that mean? Are they really as satisfied with their lives as they could be?

Or they might say, "Money isn't everything."

Now while this is certainly true, money may seem like "everything," though, for those who lack the money they need, because they're always running out of it. For them, the end of practically every month could be financially stressful. They juggle their bills and, in some cases, just make partial payments. They keep getting further and further behind and, no matter what they do, they can't seem to get ahead.

Know anybody in that situation? They might appreciate reading this book! Go ahead and share it with them. It could really help.

Some people may even go so far as to say, "I'm not materialistic," when they simply mean they can't afford something that, deep down inside, they'd really like to have. That's understandable. But the fact is, the more someone can afford to buy something, the less importance they place on material things. It's just not an issue once the money problem is out of the way.

As Jeff Bezos of Amazon.com explained in an interview with *Yahoo! Internet Life* magazine, "Once you get to a certain lifestyle, money doesn't really matter very much. Below that point, it matters tremendously."

For example, if someone's car breaks down and they don't have the money to fix it, that situation could lead to an argument, lost pay if they can't get to work, and other inconveniences. Whereas, if they had the money, it would be easy to get the car repaired, no matter what the cost. It would be no big deal; it just wouldn't matter.

Now, while it's certainly true that money can't buy happiness, one of the greatest things it does is give you options you wouldn't otherwise have. In addition to that, it also helps eliminate financial stress, which can only serve to increase your peace of mind and overall sense of well-being.

Some people put money down or criticize those with a lot of it, for whatever reason. Again, that's unfortunate.

But money is the only thing that can do what it does. As you're well aware, it buys us a home, feeds us, clothes us, builds and supports our hospitals and places of worship, and enables us to pay for our children's college educations. It also provides us with transportation, buys some of life's pleasures, and enables us to go on vacation. Besides all of that, money gives us the ability to donate to the charities of our choice.

Money isn't a luxury; it's a necessity. Without it, there's not much any of us can do. The poor can't help the poor. However, with excess money, we can do more for ourselves, as well as help those less fortunate.

Some people have a negative attitude toward money, but the truth is, money is neutral. It's just ink on paper, a medium of exchange for goods provided or services rendered. In the hands of good people, a lot of good can be done with it.

To generate more income then, you simply need to render more services or provide more goods. And this business opportunity makes available the tools and the people to help you to do that, and more.

Then there are those who say, "I don't have the time." But the fact is, we all have only 24 hours a day, and people always find time to do what's important to them. Your future success depends on how important it is to you and on how you use or invest your 24 hours to make it happen. The advantages of this business model are useless to you, unless you do something productive with it during those 24 hours.

Remember, time is your greatest personal asset. Invest it wisely! As you would do with a financial type of investment, invest some time now so you can have the potential of more time later!

Then, there are some people who honestly believe they'll do something in the future to change their lives for the better. They may say things like, "When my current situation changes," or perhaps a simple, "Someday, I'll…"

These people would like their lives to be better, and, at some level, realize they need to do something to make it so. But they put off taking any action, for whatever reason, waiting and hoping for circumstances to improve.

Sadly for them, though, virtually nothing gets better by itself. "Someday" typically turns into a new word called "never"! Until they make a decision to do something about it, and take action, their procrastination keeps them stuck in "never-never" land.

Finally, there are those who believe you can only be successful by being lucky. They spend time and money playing the lottery, or lose it to gambling. They're always hoping for success to "fall into their laps," but, of course, it just doesn't work that way.

As you've undoubtedly discovered, those who truly succeed in life don't let circumstances get in their way. They realize that there's always something going on in their lives, and that there's no "perfect" time to do anything.

Genuinely successful people always use their circumstances as reasons to move on, instead of excuses to stay where they are. That's how they became successful in the first place. They know that now is the best time to act, and they are determined to do so, no matter what.

To move further ahead in life, don't let anything or anyone stop you. After all, you're the one who has to live your life. No one can do it for you. Why not make your life more like the way you want it to be? After all, you're working hard and you deserve it.

As the saying goes, "He who hesitates is lost." Get out from under any circumstances you may have, and start imagining how your life could really be. Turn any excuses you may have for not taking action into reasons why you need to. Let your dreams for a better life tomorrow drive you forward—today.

Remember, get the best advice you can from people who really understand this business model, and watch out for any excuses, whether they're from yourself or others! Then decide what's truly right for you. Just be honest with yourself. Don't cheat yourself out of the future you would sincerely love to have.

— 11 —

"So, What Are the Main Ingredients and Advantages of an Ideal Business?" You Ask

"You need to be aware of what others are doing, applaud their efforts, acknowledge their success, and encourage them in their pursuits. When we all help one another, everybody wins."
—Jim Stovall—

Most wealthy people own a business. If you have a job, you only get paid at a wholesale rate; your employer has to make a profit on what you do. But, when you own a business—*you keep the profits!*

"So, what are some of the main ingredients and advantages of an ideal business?" you ask.

First of all, you need to be able to continue working your current occupation while you're building your business. "Don't quit your day job," is sound advice for a very good reason. Don't do anything where you could put yourself and your family in a financially risky, stressful situation where you potentially couldn't meet your daily needs.

Next, an ideal business has low overhead, with no additional rent or mortgage, and low start-up costs. You can manage it from the comfort of your home or apartment, with little or no risk. You would also have no employees to hire and support, nor would you have to deal with the other challenges they would bring. Instead, you could work with your family and friends, if you want to.

You would have no boss, no one to answer to except yourself, and no set hours.

The income potential would be great, and the prospects for expansion would be virtually limitless, with no territorial boundaries. Your business would be "portable" enabling you to build it almost anywhere in the world.

You would have access to the latest technology, but you wouldn't have to be stuck sitting in front of a computer all the time! The ideal business would also offer you low-tech options, like catalogs and toll-free ordering, for obtaining the products and services available. And you wouldn't need a computer to do that if you prefer the telephone or a fax.

You would be able to buy quality, name-brand, as well as unique consumer goods and services that are in demand, and at a discount. You would also have a money-back guarantee on them, and receive convenient deliveries right to your door.

Many of the products would be consumable, potentially leading to continuous purchasing and your earning an ongoing income. You would have a great compensation plan and receive your checks on time.

Your business would be willable to your heirs, as well as offer you certain tax advantages. There are things you would buy anyway that you could possibly use as deductions. For example, once your business income gets to a certain level, you could buy a company car with pre-tax dollars. You could also write off the portion of your home that you use for your business.

You would have a dedicated business support team of mentors and coaches who would operate with integrity, have an outstanding reputation in the marketplace, and maintain a website for your convenience.

You'd have online access to your business growth, structure, and volume, which would be carefully tracked for you and the people who team up with you. You would also have the ability to make purchases online, and your support team's website would serve as a communications tool to keep everyone informed and up to date.

You would be given the opportunity to make friends and have fun with an upbeat, positive team of people—some of whom could mentor and coach you to greater success. You would be in an environment where you'd be appropriately supported in creating and sustaining the relationships that are key to building your business. As the expression goes, "Teamwork makes the dream work."

In an ideal business, you would be encouraged, appreciated, and recognized for your accomplishments. And you would also have the opportunity to do the same for others on the team.

Regardless of the efficiency and effectiveness of the technology available in an ideal business though, no one can build greater financial security just sitting in front of a computer. As with any business, people are the most important ingredient for success. An ideal business combines high-touch with technology—the best of both worlds.

Another advantage of an ideal business is that it can be managed from home, where "click and order" replaces "bricks and mortar." The buildings, equipment, and employees of a typical business may look impressive, but they're expensive burdens you simply don't need and can't even use.

When you get right down to it, the real assets of any business are its relationships. The true success of any business is based on the relationships the business people have developed with other business people, associates, teammates, clients, customers, and the like. And it's the ability to develop new relationships that's a major factor in determining a business's growth and success.

Your mentoring and coaching team would make available a business development system of training sessions and seminars to facilitate your learning and motivation. It would also give you easy access to books, CDs, DVDs, brochures, and other materials for your personal and professional development. You wouldn't have to figure things out for yourself.

As the owner of your own business as discussed in this book, you would have all the advantages of an ideal business. You'd be enabled to pursue your life's dream, and work toward having more spare time to enjoy your family and your favorite activities.

The person who lent you this book can give you more information or refer you to an experienced leader who can help. All you need to do is ask...

But the most important ingredient of an ideal business is—*you!* No matter how good the other ingredients and advantages are, it's your utilization of them that makes it all work.

— 12 —

"But, Does This Business Model Really Work?" You May Ask

"Coming together is a beginning. Keeping together is progress. Working together is success. [And] time...spent in helping [others] to do more for themselves is far better then mere giving."
—Henry Ford—

No! Not by itself. The truth is *nothing* works by itself! And, of course, this business model doesn't work by itself either. *People* work. Buildings, equipment, and technology can't build businesses. People build businesses.

The business you're reading about is just an opportunity that people can use as a vehicle to achieve more success in their lives. And the success you achieve depends on your desire, the effort you and your team put into it, and what you're able to accomplish with it.

The truth is that it could still be done without all the advances in technology. You could still increase your financial security by using the tried and true principles of success, without ever using a computer. Countless numbers of people have already done so, before the age of the computer. But, to do so today would be much more challenging, require more time, and not allow you to be as competitive in the marketplace as you might like. Because of the Internet and advanced technologies, we now have greater capabilities and a decided advantage in managing a business.

> As a result, more people have the potential to resolve their time and money issues to the level they desire, with greater efficiency than ever before. The possibilities for expediting their success have increased because they're using the latest technological tools available, as an adjunct to the essential interpersonal relationship aspects of this business model.

In addition to technology, the support team also makes available the more traditional tools for personal and professional development that have worked for years, as discussed in the previous chapter. Those who become part of the team learn from others who are ahead of them in their journey of success, as well as those who are already where they want to be, and every level in between.

Success isn't attained simply by scrapping the old and replacing it with the new. Things aren't changed merely for the sake of change. It's keeping the traditional things that work, and incorporating the new technology to suit the needs of the times and the people using it, that is most effective.

To best support others in their quest to achieve the greatest, fastest success possible, this business model incorporates high-tech tools. However, it also uses the low-tech and high-touch foundational elements that successful businesses have used for years. This may be what initially attracted you. Perhaps, you were never interested in any kind of opportunity before. But since this one is also supported by an experienced team of mentors and coaches, you may be seriously looking at it.

Because of that, there are more people everywhere who are taking advantage of this opportunity. You may not realize it, but you may already know or have heard about some of them.

Up to this point, you've learned why this could be a great opportunity for you. You've also learned why it's so exciting, and discovered a little of what it's all about. But, as you know, unless you take what you've learned and do something with it, obviously, these are only words in a book.

As you may recall from what was said earlier, you can simply *try* this business, like test driving a car. Doesn't that make you feel more comfortable? After all, there aren't many opportunities you can just try before you would potentially make a decision to get started.

In other words, *there's no risk on your part!*

So, what would it take for you to prove to yourself that you can make this business model work for you? How many people would you be willing to share it with before you say "yes" to a better future? More importantly, are you willing to, at least, try it to find out? As Conrad Hilton said, "...the man [or woman] who wins is the [one] who tries."

Again, finish this book and ask for more details. Then simply pass it along to someone else, and watch what happens! Share this book and the opportunity it describes with as many people as you can. See for yourself how you, too, can make it work.

What could possibly happen if some of the people you lend this book to say, "Yes, I want to learn more," or, "I'm ready to go! When can I get started?" What if they team up with you and also go on to build huge businesses?

Know the answer?

You could start receiving ongoing income on the business *they* generate, which is explained in the compensation plan. It would be somewhat like being compensated for writing a song or inventing something, only you don't have to be gifted or talented to do so.

Once again, all you need to do to see if you can start making this business model work for you is to have a strong enough desire for something more in your life—*and share this opportunity with others.*

It's as simple as that.

— 13 —

So, What Is the "Secret" to Success Beyond Your Wildest Dreams?

"Desire is the key to motivation, but it's the determination and commitment to an unrelenting pursuit of your goal—a commitment to excellence—that will enable you to attain the success you seek."
— Mario Andretti —

What if embracing this business model as your own could help you achieve the life you've always wanted? Imagine what your world would be like when you've succeeded beyond your wildest dreams. Where would you be living?

What would you be doing? Who would you be spending more time with? What would you own? Where would you go? What good causes would you contribute more to?

There is one common ingredient that everyone possesses—those who enjoy a high level of success, that is...

> They've all discovered and fostered this key ingredient to be where they are today. They live wherever they want, spend time with whomever they choose, and do the things they've always wanted to do...and more.

They also have no worries about finances, and can easily meet their monthly payments, if they have any. And they can send their children to the schools and colleges of their choice.

The secret to living more successfully, beyond your wildest dreams, is really quite simple. Yet most people find themselves on such a treadmill in their everyday lives that they never discover it. They are so caught up in the "rat race," rushing from home to work and back again, that they never take the time to stop and think about it. All their friends are doing the same thing, so it seems like that's what they're supposed to do. It may be the norm, but it's far from ideal.

Some might call this activity *a rut.*

But now, you're about to learn the secret. Some of you may cast it off as too simple, while others may shake their heads in disbelief. Yet, there will be those of you who will agree. You will begin understanding that what you're being introduced to is a vehicle you can use to take you where you really want to go.

So, *believe it or not...*

The secret to success beyond your wildest dreams is to first—have wild dreams! But, before you call this "nonsense," continue reading a few more paragraphs to learn why this is true.

Like most people, you probably haven't had a massive fortune fall into your lap. Whatever you've accomplished in life so far, you've undoubtedly had to work hard for.

But, *you need to ask yourself one key question...*

Have you consciously been working toward your life-long aspirations?

As you may surmise, many people are struggling to "keep their heads above water," as the old saying goes. They're stressed out and might even feel that their life has become an exhausting grind, day in and day out. They're sick and tired of just paying bills and not getting what they really want out of life.

As you know, not all things are as they appear to be! There are many people who look good, smell good, say the right things, and may even put on a happy face, but they're really struggling. If their nice paycheck stops for 90 days, they could be in big trouble. Know anyone like that?

Guess what? They could be perfect candidates for this opportunity. After all, they don't want to lose what they have or step down from their current lifestyle. Many of them also have their kids' college bills looming on the horizon, or maybe even in their mailboxes.

So what keeps them going? Isn't it simply the thread of hope that someday their lives will be more secure? Do you know anyone in this situation?

Has it ever been a desire of yours just to have more peace of mind about things?

The trouble is, by now you may have found that your occupation, as good or high-paying as it might be, may not enable you to live or maintain the kind of life you really want.

And, like most people, it's extremely unlikely that you'll win the lottery, or inherit a large sum of money anytime soon.

The point is, very few people gain more financial security without being in a vehicle that can enable them to attain it, and without the help of a capable mentor or coach.

This business model can help you achieve some long-held dreams and goals—provided you have a desire for a better life—and take advantage of this opportunity.

Now get a pen and a sheet of paper, write down your top twenty wildest dreams, and don't hold back. With them solidly before you, you can start working toward their achievement by diligently applying yourself to this vehicle. Setbacks and obstacles may slow you down, but you won't let them stop you.

When you know where you're headed, and you have a solid business support team behind you, you're more inclined to keep going. Focus on what you really want, and continue doing what you need to do to accomplish your goals. You'll then create the momentum you need to achieve the greater success to which you aspire.

Your wildest dreams can drive you to take the next step, and then the next. In time, you could find yourself getting closer and closer to making each of them come true, and to living the life you really want to live.

When you get back with the person who shared this book with you, you can learn from them, or someone on the support team, how to make this opportunity work for you.

Now, while learning "how" is important, knowing "why" you want or need to do it is the only reason you'll ever do it. A sincere desire to make your wildest dreams come true is a starting point to begin your quest to do so. A strong reason why would be the driving force behind making progress toward realizing your wildest dreams.

Makes sense, doesn't it?

It may come as a surprise to you, but most people don't resolve their time and money issues because they're highly educated, gifted, or talented. They simply have a strong enough desire to do so, and take the necessary action to reach their goals. Along the way, they resolve their time and money issues so they can live their dreams. They apply themselves in a vehicle that has the potential of giving them the results they're looking for.

What do you want out of your one and only life, anyway? Have you seriously thought about that lately? Are you tired of the "rat race" you may be in; packing in a lot of activity but not really getting where you want to go?

Now ask yourself the following four questions, and you'll discover the right answers—*for you*:

1) So what *are* your wildest dreams? If you haven't already done so, take out a piece of paper and write them down now.

2) Would you really like to see them come true?

3) Do you respect yourself enough to do whatever it takes to give yourself the life you want?

4) Isn't it time for you to make your move, and do something that is capable of giving you the results you so earnestly want and deserve?

"*Those who have attained things worth having in this world have worked while others idled, have persevered when others gave up in despair, have practiced early in life the valuable habits of self-denial, industry, and singleness of purpose. As a result, they enjoy the success so often erroneously attributed to good luck.*"

—Grenvill Kleiser

— 14 —

No, No, a Thousand Times No!

*"First, there are those who are
winners and they know they are winners...Then
there are those who aren't yet winners, but they don't
quit. They're the ones for me. They never quit trying.
They're the soul of our game."*
— Bear Bryant —

He was turned down over 1,000 times by some of the best restaurant people in the world, before he even started to succeed. So, you might be asking, "What could I possibly learn from someone who's been rejected over 1,000 times?"

Nothing, if you don't want to! But you might want to take a lesson from someone who, after more than 1,000 noes, was not willing to let those rejections stop him from pursuing his objective.

To help yourself move on, you may need to pay attention to someone who kept taking just one more chance to see his dream come true.

You just might learn something from someone who absolutely refused to quit, until he got a "yes," which occurred after 1,009 noes. He was 66-years-old when he started!

Colonel Sanders, of KFC (Kentucky Fried Chicken) fame, was one of those people who just kept on going, in spite of all the challenges. By doing so, he started one of the most successful fast food restaurant chains in the world.

There are probably others, closer to you, who have lived through many rejections, yet they continue pursuing their dreams and goals. These people could help you achieve yours as well. So, who are they?

One of them could be the person who lent you this book! *But only if you ask.*

They believe you have the potential and, hopefully, a sincere desire to be even more successful. And, like Colonel Sanders, they keep on going until they create the life they want. They don't let anyone or anything stand in their way.

They're just doing whatever it takes to get the results they want.

How about you?

When you get back with the person who you received this book from, share some of your wildest dreams and goals. They, or one of their support team members, can help you put together an action plan. They can assist you in getting on the path to truly resolving your time and money issues, achieving more, and attaining greater financial security.

As mentioned earlier, examine and evaluate this opportunity. Also know that it's okay to be skeptical about something new. In fact, it's strongly recommended. Let that healthy caution make you look really hard at what you are considering here.

When you see the potential this business model could represent for you, you just might fall in love with your wildest dreams. *Congratulations!*

Go ahead and dream. You now have a real opportunity, and a vehicle with which you can make your dreams come true.

Go ahead and do it. Other people have done it to make their wildest dreams come true, and you can too.

"*Opportunity can benefit no one who has not fitted themselves to seize it and use it. Opportunity woos the worthy, but shuns the unworthy. Prepare yourself to grasp opportunity and opportunity is likely to come your way. It is not so fickle, capricious, and unreasoning as some say.*"

— B.C. Forbes

—15—
If Only I Had
Taken the Chance…When
It Came Along

*"If your life is ever going to get better, you'll
have to take a chance. There is simply no way you can
grow—without taking chances."*
— David Viscot —

As they say, hindsight is always 20/20. At the
beginning of this book, you read about a
man who went to work for Microsoft,
bought some stock, and became a millionaire. He
couldn't possibly have known that would have

happened to him! He just believed in the company and the opportunity for himself to create wealth with it.

Would you have bought some Microsoft stock, as well, back in the early days?

Another gentleman, from Maryland, had some money to invest. He found a small bank that was selling shares for only a dollar each and bought 25,000. In a few years, that same bank was taken over at a price of almost $22 a share. On a $25,000 investment, he received over $550,000!

Where could you get that kind of "inside" information? More importantly, what if you were able to gain some additional insight concerning the future and the possibilities for you with this innovative business model? Would you do anything about it?

We've all heard rags-to-riches stories like these before. In fact, you may have already passed on some other opportunities, prior to this one coming into your life, which you are now considering.

For example, Wal-Mart, McDonalds, and others have made rich people out of many early believers. At that time, most had only a hunch and some faith that they would do well with these companies.

But, it wasn't the information they were given that made them wealthy…

It was what they did with that information that made the difference in their lives. It was the opportunity they took advantage of that helped them realize their dreams.

So now, what are you going to do with the information you've just learned? Are you going to use it to make a difference in your life as well as in the lives of others?

Are you going to take this chance to grow and make your dreams come true—like the people you've just read about?

Armed with the 20/20 foresight you've just developed, will you use it to your advantage?

You now have some "inside" information that can help you resolve your time and money issues and achieve greater financial security. But what you do with it is entirely up to you.

"When you have a sense of your own identity and a vision of where you want to go in your life, you then have the basis for reaching out to the world and going after your dreams for a better life."

—Stedman Graham

— 16 —

Now's the Time to Earnestly Pursue Living Your Dream! This Just Might Be Your Chance…

"My will shall shape the future. Whether I fail or succeed shall be no [one's]doing but my own. I am the force; I can clear any obstacle before me or I can be lost in the maze. My choice; my responsibility; win or lose, only I hold the key to my destiny."
— Elaine Maxwell —

You are now at a crossroad. You now have some information about an exciting cutting edge business opportunity that could have a tremendous impact on your future. But this is only the beginning…

As you know by now, more information is available. The point is, you can get whatever you need to make an informed decision.

However, without a decision to take action, all you have here is some information. If you do nothing with it, you will gain nothing from it. And, as with any other opportunity, there are no guarantees of success. Fortunately, though, it doesn't just depend solely on you and your efforts. You'll have a support team to assist you.

But, once again, ask yourself, "If I keep doing what I'm now doing, where will I be in the next two to five years?"

Will you be living the life you truly aspire to or honestly be satisfied with the status-quo? Will you start investing some time now to work toward generating the additional income you may want or need to better secure your future? If you're now living paycheck to paycheck and not really where you want to be in life, will that be acceptable to you in the long-run?

According to a study by a large insurance company, most people use 95% of their disposable income to service their debt load. That sure doesn't leave much money with which to build a secure future, now does it?

Again, if you have a sincere desire to move on in life, get back with the person who shared this book with you. Meet some people, ask some questions, learn more, and give it a try.

Imagine the possibilities for yourself and your family. This just might be the opportunity you've been looking for—the one you could use to move forward.

So, *what other viable options might you have?*

Will you forego yet another chance, and let this opportunity slip through your fingers? Will you be like the millions of people who didn't invest in Microsoft and didn't benefit from its growth?

Or, will you act now and do *something*, whether it's taking advantage of this opportunity or not, to take more control of your destiny?

As you know, you're the only one who can decide how much you want your dreams to come true. And you're the only one who can take the steps necessary to make it happen for you and your family.

So, *what are you going to do?*

You could now be holding the key to the opportunity of a lifetime, right in the palm of your hand. But what are you going to do about it?

You may want to read this book again and think—*really stop and think*—about your life so far and how satisfied you may really be.

Are you completely happy with where you are? Or, would you like to accomplish more? Would you like to do some of the things you've always dreamed of, but your current occupation isn't structured in such a way that you can do them?

Granted, nothing is for everybody. But take a moment and imagine having the time and money to truly live your dream. Imagine spending time with positive, enthusiastic people who are on the way or already have their time and money issues resolved, and can help you do the same.

Before they started taking advantage of this business model, they may have been doing as well or better than you are. But something was missing in their lives, so they seized this opportunity. And now, you've been given the chance to join their ranks. Who knows? After you meet some of them you may find yourself saying, "Count me in!"

Success-oriented people are always open to opportunity, and apply themselves to a vehicle that's capable of rewarding them appropriately for their efforts. If they're doing something that's not producing the results they want, they transition into doing something else that can. It's that simple and it's just a choice.

Now you may ask, "What are the odds I can resolve my time and money issues with this opportunity?" But *the most important question is to ask yourself...*

"What are the odds I'll resolve my time and money issues if I don't take advantage of this opportunity?"

Are you finally going to pursue more of your dreams? Are you finally going to pursue the life you really, really want?

Are you sick and tired of being sick and tired, and ready to say "I've had enough! Now it's my turn, and I'm going to do something about it."

As suggested earlier, honestly answer these two simple questions...

1) If you're not going to take advantage of this opportunity to work toward resolving your time and money issues, then what will you do to live your dream?

And...

2) If you don't do something now, will you be sorry later?

*   *   *

To learn more about how you can use the power of this innovative business model to potentially resolve your time and money issues and work toward living your dream, contact the person who lent you this book:

Name_____

Phone (_____**)**_____**e-mail**_____

Street_____

City_____**State**_____**Zip**_____

*   *   *

Now Go Share This Book with Others...
and Watch What Happens!

"*So, what are you going to do to better secure your financial future, now that you've been given the chance? Will you pass on working toward resolving your time and money issues? Or...will you take action, do* something *to accelerate your success...and make your dreams come true?*"

— John Fuhrman